Where Was God in All of This?
Encouragement for Young Women

By: Shaniece J. Miller

In dedication and sweet loving memory to my grandmother and great grandmothers:

Katherine, Mattie, and Martha

Grandmothers and roses are much the same. Each are God's masterpieces with different names.

-- Author Unknown

"Your heartaches, pain, trials and struggles can serve as someone else's hope. If you make it through, somebody else is going to make it through. Tell your story."

~Shaniece Miller

Foreword

To My Most Dearest Beloved; Shaniece Jacole Miller

I Love You. I am so proud of you; I have a joy in my heart that is unexplainable.

On September 29, 1985 at 10:18am, Sunday morning my life changed and has never been the same. On this day God allowed me to give birth to the best blessing that I could have ever received in my life, you were born! Fresh out of my womb, Dr. Kakarla handed you to me, I looked into your small beautiful face, tears began to flow, I could not believe you were finally here, my most precious jewel. I snuggled, kissed and held you close to my heart. My grandmother (Mama Dear) walked over to my bed and said to me, "Shelia, I expect you to raise this child right and make sure she knows who God is". As tears of joy and uncertainty fell from my eyes, I whispered a prayer of thanksgiving and protection over your life, and I asked God to show me how to take care of you and to be the best mother I could be to you. And God did just what I asked Him to do. As we journeyed through this life together, we have had high and lows, but we never left one another, we made the best out of every situation that came into our lives together. And we made it baby, God has truly blessed and anointed you through all of your trials and pain, heartaches, tears and setbacks, He has and ordained your story for such a time as this. Even when you or I did not understand, He was there! As I read your book, He revealed Himself through YOU to me. During some deep depression as I encountered while in my marriage, nights when I felt all alone, you climbed in bed with me, I felt your slender arms around me and your cheeks pressing against my face, He was there! As you heard the doctors reported a death diagnosis over my life, through your pain and tears, you climbed in bed with me and began to pray healing over my life, rebuked every evil plot of the devils' lie, He was there! Wanting to drop out of college to take care of me, not knowing if you could stay focused on your college education, He was there! The many, many surprise trips home just to check on me. He was there! The prayers, encouragement and tears you shared with me during the death of my Loved Ones, my Grandmother, my fiancée', my father, and most recent, my mother, He was there! And at times being with me just for the sake of a good laugh together, He was there! And when YOU tried to be my MOTHER, He was there! LOL!!!!

Boops, thank you for being a child that listened, followed and applied what you were being taught. I know it didn't make sense at times, but as you grew in your relationship with God, and had to trust Him not for me, but for yourself, you soon realized that He was there all the time. Congratulations on your many accomplishments, including your soon-to-be DOCTORIAL DEGREE, and the success of this book. He is STILL here with US.

In advance, I celebrate the many lives that your story will help break free of any emotional chains holding them back. Thank you for your transparency and truth; you are an amazing Woman of God.

Seek His face, and keep the Faith.

Forever in Love with You.

Mommy

Shelia Jones Venters

The Foundation

Growing up, I never liked being an only child. That might sound cliché', but it's the truth! I always experienced two birthday parties, two Christmas celebrations, and never really having to share anything. My parents were young when they had me, so I never got to experience the "family" life with my biological parents. For as long as I can remember, it was just me and my mom. My dad was always in my life and was a wonderful daddy and still is but I lived in the house with my mother. When we first moved into our own place, we really didn't have anything. A mattress, couple of pieces of furniture, a few dishes, and clothes. I was really young when all of this happened, but what makes me remember the details so vividly is the peace and contentment that my mother had. We literally had next to nothing, but she was at peace. Her mind was at rest, and she loved me with everything that she had which was enough to fill every room in our empty apartment. At such a young age, my mother had a grace about herself that I still can remember. I really didn't know what it was about her then because my young mind couldn't comprehend such depth, but now that I am older, I understand. I get it! That same grace as a young mother has followed her into her years as a mother of a young adult. There is an aurora of grace, excellence, greatness, beauty, and divinity that surrounded her and kept her intact while raising a young child. My father, since I was a young child, has always had a love for me that is indescribable. There is an amazing connection that my Father and I have anytime that I am feeling sad, depressed, or upset, all I have to do is call my daddy! He always knows what to say. Even if he has to do it with "tough love" it is just what I need. Whenever he is around me, I would always feel a spirit of protection and security. There was never a time that I can't remember feeling this way when I was in his presence. My father has always been a hard worker and because of the example that he set for me, those same qualities have remained with me into my adult years. My father is the coolest, laid back, chill type of guy and I love it. He is a thinker. Always thinking ahead. Always moving forward. He is smart! I admire his work ethic so much that I have adapted many things from being in his presence. Every time I would be in the car with my father, he would always make me read road signs. He would ask me intellectual questions. Keep me updated with current events. Somewhere between the ages of 8-10 my daddy would take me out on back roads and teach me how to drive his car. I know that was illegal, but it was fun and at the age of 15 I knew how to drive, had my first car and a driver's license. I really didn't understand why my daddy would make me do a lot of things so young. I used to think that it was because he didn't have a son so he would make me do things that young boys did at my age. But as I grew up and begin to experience life for myself, I realized that my daddy was laying a foundation for me to become and do anything that I wanted to do, without depending on others and to know how to educate myself if I didn't know the answer. He was setting me up to succeed even though I was unaware at that time in my life. As I have looked back in retrospect, my daddy taught me lessons that only a father can teach his daughter. The respect that I have for my father is due to the firm foundation, morals, and life lessons that he laid when I was just a child. Being a young adult, I have come to the realization that our heavenly Father is the same way! He wants to establish a solid intimate relationship in our youth so that we will be able to help our children and their children become all that they can be. I have a tremendous amount of respect for both of my parents! Both of them were popular, intelligent, all American athlete's, went to college on athletic scholarships, and gave all of that up to become parents. Their lives were put on hold, so that I could grow up and enjoy the life that I have now! Sometimes I think about what my parents' lives would have been like if they would have decided to not allow me to come into the world. But quickly God reminds me that *ALL things work together for the good to them that love God, to them who are called according to his purpose.* I am here for a purpose and no other individuals but my parents could have created me. That was part of their purpose! It was all according to His perfect plan.

February 14th

February 3rd, one of my most favorite days of each year, my mom's birthday! I never had a problem remembering my parents' birthday because they were on the same day! My dad's in January and my mom's in February, both on the 3rd. Lucky right? Absolutely! I never would have thought that one of my most favorite days would become one of the scariest yet profound days in my life! On February 3rd, 2006, my mom's birthday, she was diagnosed with renal failure. I begin to tear up as I write this because I remember the way my body felt and how dizzy I became when the doctor literally looked my mother in the face and told her, "Ms. Venters, we do not know how you are alive right now because both of your kidneys have shut down and you will have to go on dialysis immediately!" I cried in the ER room like I never have before! I lost it! Like seriously! This is my mother! MY MOTHER! My rock! My love! My role model! My hero! My everything! At that moment, I began to verbally voice my hatred and anger towards her ex-husband. You see my mother was married for 12 years to a man that I had grown to love and respect. For many years we had what most would call the "ideal" family. My step-father, mom, step-sister, and myself. Our house was the "go-to" house for all of my family and friends! Both parents served in the church. My step-sister and I never really wanted for anything. Now that I look back, it was "ideal." Lies, cheating, deceit, infidelity, and a BOZO of a man drove what was once an "ideal" marriage and family apart. My step-fathers actions does not negate the fact that ALL marriage relationships have their highs and lows, and neither party entering the marriage relationship is perfect, however, I knew that my mother was a modern day Proverbs 31 woman! She was virtuous and faithful to her husband and family! She was a mother to many! Not only did she accept and respond to my step-sister as if she birthed her, but to my friends, cousins and even her friends as well! She taught us the ways of our Father in heaven. She was always of service to others! Whether at church in the different ministries that she served in, in our school athletic activities that we were a part of. My mother knew that marriage and family was just as much work as it is lovely. She worked for her family, in deed, in time, as well as finances. She made sure that her family's needs were put before and met before her own! If you have never read the story of the Proverbs 31 woman, stop reading my book right now and pick up your bible, kindle, iPad, phone, or whatever you use to access the bible and read Proverbs 31:10-31! This was and is my mother today!!! The nasty, painful, heart-rending divorce drove my mother to a level of stress and discontentment. Everything that she had so diligently worked for in her marriage and family was taken away. The very thing that brought her so much joy, happiness, and peace was now anguishing, agonizing, and LITERALLY taking the life out of her! At the age of 40, a young beautiful, God-fearing, loving, faithful, spiritual woman was dying of a broken heart! I could never imagine on my birthday, being told that I was dying! This is the day that family and friends celebrate your existence! This day regardless of age, is supposed to be full of laughs, gifts, remember when, new goals, gratefulness, and telling everyone how good it feels to be 21 for the thousandth time! But on this day, February 3rd, the day my mother was born, she was dying physically. My mother reminded me of the Shunammite woman in the bible. Just like the Shunammite woman, my mother was able to minister to me while in misery!

18 When the child had grown, he went out one day to his father among the reapers. 19 And he said to his father, "Oh, my head, my head!" The father said to his servant, "Carry him to his mother." 20 And when he had lifted him and brought him to his mother, the child sat on her lap till noon, and then he died. 21 And she went up and laid him on the bed of the man of God and shut the door behind him and went out. 22 Then she called to her husband and said, "Send me one of the servants and one of the donkeys that I may quickly go to the man of God and come back again." 23 And he said, "Why will you go to him today? It is neither new moon nor Sabbath." She said, "All is well." 24 Then she saddled the donkey, and she said to her servant, "Urge the animal on; do not slacken the pace for me unless I tell you." 25 So she set out and came to the man of God at Mount Carmel.

When the man of God saw her coming, he said to Gehazi his servant, "Look, there is the Shunammite. 26 Run at once to meet her and say to her, 'Is all well with you? Is all well with your husband? Is all well with the child?'" And she answered, "All is well." 27 And when she came to the mountain to the man of God, she caught hold of his feet. And Gehazi came to push her away. But the man of God said, "Leave her alone, for she is in bitter distress, and the Lord has hidden it from me and has not told me." 28 Then she said, "Did I ask my lord for a son? Did I not say, 'Do not deceive me?'?" 29 He said to Gehazi, "Tie up your garment and take my staff in your hand and go. If you meet anyone, do not greet him, and if anyone greets you, do not reply. And lay my staff on the face of the child." 30 Then the mother of the child said, "As the Lord lives and as you yourself live, I will not leave you." So he arose and followed her. 31 Gehazi went on ahead and laid the staff on the face of the child, but there was no sound or sign of life. Therefore he returned to meet him and told him, "The child has not awakened."

32 When Elisha came into the house, he saw the child lying dead on his bed. 33 So he went in and shut the door behind the two of them and prayed to the Lord. 34 Then he went up and laid on the child, putting his mouth on his mouth, his eyes on his eyes, and his hands on his hands. And as he stretched himself upon him, the flesh of the child became warm. 35 Then he got up again and walked once back and forth in the house, and went up and stretched himself upon him. The child sneezed seven times, and the child opened his eyes. 36 Then he summoned Gehazi and said, "Call this Shunammite." So he called her. And when she came to him, he said, "Pick up your son." 37 She came and fell at his feet, bowing to the ground. Then she picked up her son and went out.

The deathly and decaying experience that was going on around her did not reflect the determined expectation of God that was within her! My mother responded to my reaction of her situation just like the Shunammite woman did when the servant Gehazi asked her *"Is all well with you?"* My mother looked at me with a smile on her face and said *ALL IS WELL WITH ME!* I know what the doctors have said, I know what it looks like, but my God specializes in healing the sick, raising the dead, and performing miracles! *ALL IS WELL!* I was saved at this time, but I was also a babe in Christ. My young 22 year old mind could not wrap around the fact that my mother smiled so eloquently, with so much peace, grace, and certainty that she was well! Just like the Shunammite woman, she knew that her son was dead before she responded to the servant, but she also knew the man she was going to speak with about the situation! That is a lesson for all of us. Even though my mother knew she was dying before the doctors came in, she had an intimate relationship with the MAN that she was going to talk to about her situation. Regardless of what things may look like, when you seem to have "dead" situations in your life, when you know the MAN to talk too, you can respond by saying *ALL IS WELL WITH ME* in the midst of! WOW! That just gave me hope all over again!! September 8th, 2006 my mother received a kidney transplant! Not much information was given to us about the donor; however, the small amount of information was very profound! The donor was 22 years old, the same age that I was at the time. He died instantly from a motorcycle accident. He resided upstate, my mother and I live in Texas. The part of the story that still gives me chills even today is that the donor was an EXACT match! The doctors were in disbelief that this person was not a family member or that the donor was not her own child! At that time, I was the same age of the donor, and biologically my mother's child, I was not a match! At this moment, for any reason, if you have any limits on what God can do, TAKE THEM OFF!! Only such actions could come from a powerful, limitless, splendid, all knowing creator! God has a way of making ALL THINGS WORK TOGETHER! If that didn't give you chills keep reading! As I stated earlier, I am an only child so I am the sole beneficiary for my mother. Before her surgery, I had to do some of the hardest things that I have ever done. The doctor needed my signature on my mother's will. I was informed that this surgery is life threatening and that it was no guarantee, that her body could possibly reject the new kidney and that she may not come out alive. The surgery would last anywhere from 6-8 hours the doctors said, so I camped out, {literally} in the waiting room. I remember praying to God like never before. My mother was all that I had! Before going into the surgery, she told the doctors to let her talk to me in private. The words that my mother spoke to me in that hospital room have been some of the most influential words that has carried me and gotten me through some of the darkest times in my life. She looked at me said so eloquently "regardless of what happens in that room, the treasures, gifts, and your knowledge of Christ that I have instilled in you, is more important than the outcome of my surgery. I know that if I die today, you will continue to live a blessed and successful life, because I have already entrusted you in the hands of my Father in Heaven. You will continue be the young woman for Christ that you are destined to be!" *ALL IS WELL!* That was the first time in my life that I experienced such peace in a painful situation. Here is my mother, lying on the hospital bed, in a life or death situation, speaking life into me! Helping me to reassure my faith by pouring wisdom into me, my mother reaffirmed her faith and remained faithful to her Father. Though she was slain, she yet still trusted Jesus! And not only did she trust Him in such a dark and dismal time, she dared me to do the same! 3 ½-4 hours into the surgery, I received a phone call from the doctors inside of the surgery room. My heart dropped, I am sure I went blind temporarily; I don't even think I said hello. The time on the clock did not reflect the length of the surgery that the doctors informed me of before my mother went in. I knew she was gone. God where are you? Why? The nurse on the other end of the phone was informing me that the surgery was over and that my mother was ALIVE and WELL! She said that this was the first time that a transplant had taken this short amount of time because my mother had less than 3% body fat! She was alive, everything was great, and she was asking for me! I did not know that my mother had taken a picture of me in the surgery room with her. The nurse said that when she woke up, she looked right at the place where it was! I get emotional thinking about it all over again. There is no question as to where God was in all of this! He was in the same place then as He is now! RIGHT HERE with us! If you noticed, I titled this chapter a specific date but I started it off with a completely different date. That wasn't by accident, but to further put you in awe of the God I serve.

February 3rd, 2006-diagnosed with renal/kidney failure

{Mom's birthday}

February 14th, 2006- First Day of Dialysis

September 8th, 2006- SUCCESSFUL kidney transplant

Like my mother and the Shunammite woman, be encouraged that all problems have a beginning, middle, and end date! Be encouraged that whatever you may be facing whether you are just now starting to go through it, you are in the middle of it, or you can see sunshine at the end of the tunnel, IT WILL END! God has a date for the "dead" things in your life. In all of His infinite wisdom, He has a way of working things out that you know without a doubt it was Him! There is nothing you could have done, said, or even thought about doing to bring you out what was designed to destroy you. There is no struggle, trial, tribulation, nasty divorce, sickness, or disease that God will not face with you. Eight years later, at 48 years of age, my mother is as healthy as she has ever been! And to expose that God has a sense of humor, she has her own business, "Divine Fitness" where she serves as a licensed personal trainer! Where was God? Right there through it all! At the hospital, in the surgery room, at the dialysis center, holding her at night while she was restless from all of the turmoil and tragedy that was going on, with me at college trying to process it all, with the family who lost their son in the motorcycle accident, with our family and friends! *ALL IS WELL*

Sandpaper

At this point in my life, "I thought" I would be married, a kid or two, serving my husband and my family. I hear often that if you want to make God laugh, tell Him your plans. Well I am sure he is rolling on the floors of heaven, kicking His feet, stomach in knots, laughing at me and "my plans". I had it all planned out: Graduate college, get married two years later. Have at least one kid and break the news to my husband that he had hit another homerun! {That was a good one}. Three years later, I am still single, no kids, and no one is up to bat! I am sure like many of you, encountered that one person who you just knew was "the one". They were a heaven sent angel! Your modern day "Boaz". If you have never been to a college football game in Texas, please put that on your bucket list right now. He was the star player on the football team and I was the captain on the dance team! Perfectly matched popular couple huh? WRONG! Modern day "Saved by the Bell" couple? NOT! If ever I have heard the voice of God so clearly, it was on this day. DO NOT DATE HIM. So clear! Crystal clear! And I knew! It gave me chills! Now when I reflect back on this relationship with my ex-boyfriend, I know that it's not the fact that he was a bad person or meant to harm me intentionally, he just wasn't ready for what I thought I needed, and I didn't need to endure all of the issues and situations that was coming along with our relationship. I also had to do a lot of self-evaluation and understand that I played a huge role in the defeat of my relationship. I am sure like many of you have tried "to save" or "fix" your man. I discovered that I was an enabler. I was the one who heard God's voice before entering the relationship and when I decided to pursue it, God didn't stop talking to me! I thought that I could save him and make him be the man that I wanted and needed to be. The last time I checked, Jesus was the only SAVIOR that we have. Instead of allowing God to come into both of our lives and heal our hurtful places, I tried to "handle it." Just call me Shaniece Pope! (Scandal Fans). I decided to pursue what I wanted to do instead of being obedient to God and two days later, I was changing my relationship status from single to "in a relationship" on Facebook and MySpace. I was in a previous relationship for almost two years only to discover that another young lady and I were sharing the same young man as our "boyfriend". Needless to say, I was going through the "I can't be alone phase." I didn't know how valuable and what a gift I was to the Kingdom of God as a young single woman! I didn't know that in my singleness I was trusted with undistracted time. I didn't know that this is the place that God could get the best out of me. I didn't know that this was my opportunity to serve other people, become the young woman of God that I was destined to be and that I had so much free time to get back to me. I didn't know those things because for two years, the security of my relationship with my boyfriend was what I thought I needed. After everything I had gone through with my mother, he along with his mother was right by my side and I will always be grateful for that. It is ok to turn to others in times of despair, and God will send people your way to comfort you, but it is in those dark, desperate times that God is looking for us to throw ourselves at His feet. Pour out your heart and allow Him to rock you ever so sweetly in His loving arms. *Matthew 11:28 says "come to me, all you who are weary and burdened, and I will give you rest."* Not only can you come to God in your discontented moments, but you can rest, not sleep, but rest! Only God has the power to give you rest when your situations are rigid. To be able to rest in a rigid place is evident of God's power in your life. Nothing is straight, everywhere you turn has a sharp cutting edge ready to slice you and prick you with the issues of life, but when you allow God to take control, you will rest in the most reeling of places in your life. As I look back now, I know that God placed me on my college team because I am an awesome dancer and that was a desire of my heart, but more so for the lives that I touched as being the leader of my team at that time. Even today, when I talk to my ex-teammates, they share with me how thankful they are for me and the knowledge and truth that I shared with them whenever hard times would arise in their lives. I can honestly say that God used me to inspire and encourage the lives of the young women that were under my authority at that time while in my brokenness and those experiences, friendships, and moments I will always cherish. It was in those moments that I had to minister to my teammates while going through hell in my relationship, that God was calling me for greater purposes. Things with my boyfriend were great at times. He was a couple of years younger than me, but his presence took away the pain and hurt from my past relationship. The one that I still wasn't healed from! It was new, fresh, and I found myself moving on and really falling back into being in a relationship. Let's take a life pause right here: Getting under a new man/woman will NOT help you get over the old one! That is a place that only God can heal. It's a hurtful place that only God has the pain remedy for. Yes, God did send other people to help, encourage, inspire, and motivate me from the heartbreak of that relationship, but people are limited to how much they can help you. God will reach down deep, scrape away all of the sadness, mend the mess, heal your heart, and then write you a prescription to medicate the masses with your message! Ok. Unpause. Things were great! He made me laugh, we did things that I like to do, he supported my dance team events, he bought me things, we went out, and he knew my favorites and dislikes. From the outside in, everything looked like your "ideal" college relationship. We went to church together, bible study for college athletes on Tuesdays, and even personal bible studies at home. For about four months into my relationship, I forgot that I was ever in one before entering this. When the enemy paints a picture, you can believe that it is only so long before the value of the artist and the artwork is revealed. Slowly but surely, the art began to fade, chip, and the artist was beginning to show that he was nothing more than an amateur. For the sake of repetition the young man whom I thought was a modern day BOAZ turned out to be nothing more than a BOZO. Please understand that this is not a "bash my ex" chapter of the book. I have already gotten that out of my system years ago, and he and I have received forgiveness from all that happened between both of us, however, every circumstance that I had to encounter has shaped me into the young woman that I am today, and all of this is coming from a HEALED place in my life. However, someone may be reading this and you could possibly identify and relate to some of the same characteristics that are going on in your relationship and life. If so, leave this clown before ALL of his jokes are on you! In public, the "mask" was on. He "performed" and put on a show in front of others. The picture was painted of a well, functional relationship to others, but no one really saw what it was when the "makeup" came off. When I heard God's voice telling me not to date him, I should have known that at that moment, God was only doing one of the many things that He does so well: PROTECT his children. When you are disobedient to God's word, the enemy will trick you and entice you to think that the decision you made was better than God's! God can't possibly give me the best, so I have to do things on my own. When God says no, He means it! Men tend to be very predictable human beings. They have a pattern, a routine. When things are out of place and the norm changes in their daily pattern, our God given gift to women, intuition will kick in. The lies started. Text messages, secretive phone calls, lock codes on the phone, condoms hidden in the glove compartment, pictures of me hidden in the car under the arm rest. I know you are probably thinking that these things happen all the time in relationships when the other person isn't serious about being committed. And you may further think that there is nothing "out of the norm" or extreme with these behaviors. The difference here is I KNEW I wasn't supposed to be in this relationship. But when you decide to pursue your will instead of God's, even when you KNOW, at this point the enemy has made it so hard for you to come out of the situation. I felt like my flesh and faith were playing tug-o-war with my mind! I knew what I wanted to do, but I also knew what God was trying to get me not to do. I was gone! Lost all in the sauce and that is exactly where the enemy wanted me. God knew that this would happen that's why He said not to date him. The enemy knew that as long as I was in that toxic relationship, I would not be able to tell the good news of Christ. Other women started calling me, my friends telling me things, his room smelling like a woman's fragrance that I didn't wear. At this point you are probably thinking, why did you stay with him that long? You should have left! And if you are thinking that, you are right! I was in so deep. I never allowed myself to totally heal from my previous relationship, so I ended up covering up a wound with an emotional Band-Aid. Sex was the isopropyl alcohol and liquor was the peroxide. I thought that I could surely heal with these elements in my life. In order for a wound to heal, you have to assess it with the right remedies. The more you keep it covered without taking the necessary steps, the longer it takes to heal. My heart was open, my feelings were wounded and instead of allowing God to come in and bring me back to Himself, I tried to "nurse" myself back to health when in reality all I really did was make the wound worse, allowing it to get infected with another inconsistent, immature, irrational man. As I stated earlier, women notice patterns that our men have. I knew things were off with him. I knew that his attention was being diverted. His response to me was different. At this moment, I am sure like many other women have, I tried to "please" him in ways that would make him happy and get the pattern back to normal. Smoking, drinking, pornography, video games, and even more sex became a part of my "pattern" only to end up feeling used, lower than low and unappreciated. Please note that I have always been independent, hardworking, God-fearing and about my business. However, the enemy does not care how much of a "boss" you are! As a matter of fact, the enemy seeks individuals like me to destroy. *John 10:10 says "the thief comes only to steal, kill and destroy."* It does not give a particular type of person, gender, height, financial status; NO ONE is exempt from the snares and schemes of Satan. That's why the bible tells us in *Proverbs 4:23 to "above all else, guard your heart, for everything you do flows from it."* The day that I heard God's voice telling me not to pursue this relationship, is the day that God was ready and willing to collect all of the broken pieces from my heart and put it back together again, while giving the second half of John 10:10 *"I have come that they may have life and have it more abundantly"*. God was ready to give me life. He was ready to heal me but I chose to take the easy way out and hindered my healing for four years. Because I couldn't understand why God wouldn't want me with such a great guy, I used my limited perspective on life. I made a life decision based on limited data. God knows all and sees all. He can see into the minds and hearts of men. He can see the future because He is already there. He knew that all of this would happen to me. *No good thing will He withhold from those who walk uprightly {Psalms 84:11}* is an indicator that God has our best interest at heart. Arguments, fights, items being broken, windows being busted, hurtful words being exchanged became the weekly norm for two people who were hurting. I was hurting from the relationship that I was previously in and never healed from and he was hurting from the relationship that he never had: with his mother. I am a strong believer that women cannot teach boys how to be men.

There is always that piece of the make-up of man that is missing when he does not have a relationship with his Father. While the world is ever so busy teaching our young men to how to be "hard", never show emotion, never let anyone see you cry, a mother of a son is equipped with gifts and grace to complete the missing piece. She has the privilege to show him how to love and be loved. She shows him how to treat and care for a woman. She can instill in him the values and behaviors that only a woman can communicate to a man. She allows her son to be her protector so that his woman will feel safe when she is with him. A mother to a son shows him how to be gentle and not soft. A mother shows him correct mannerisms all the while allowing him to be a young man. That's the power that women have. I have so much respect for the mothers who have sons in the fathers absence because typically the son has a love and respect for his mother that exudes from him. She is patient with her son so therefore, in essence she is non-verbally communicating to him that you do not have to get things right the first time, you will make mistakes, learn from them and keep pushing. When a mother is so in tune with her son and they have a solid relationship, regardless of what life or puberty may throw at them, he will respect her. If a man can learn to respect his mother he will know how to respect his woman. My ex- boyfriend did not have a solid relationship with his mother. Arguments and her marriage caused separation between the two. There were many conversations between the two of us about how he felt about his mother. I could always see in his eyes the yearning for her love and acceptance. He loved her and wanted so badly for her to return the same love to him. Hurt people, hurt people! His inward anguish became his outward actions. Due to everything that he lacked with his mother, he sought out in me and other women. Every void that he had, he tried to fill it with fantasies from other females. I knew. I could tell. I was in so deep. Every time I would leave, I found myself always going back. I can't tell you how many times I left over the course of four years. Digging myself deeper into the emotional pit that started four years ago. Getting drunk at least twice a week. Going to class and work drunk or hung over depending on what the episode was about that week. This was not me. I had gotten so wrapped up in him, that I totally lost me. My eyes were blinded with bitterness, my ears were clogged with confusion, my hands were tied from not being healed and the device that the devil uses, depression, begin to deceive me into thinking I wasn't good enough and taking my own life was my only way out. I had to be with him if I was alive so, the only way I could get out of this was to end my life. I literally watched myself go from a young, beautiful, outgoing, God fearing woman to becoming low, bitter, unhappy, harsh, miserable, and despondent. God knew that not only was I not ready to be in this relationship, he wasn't either. When the Holy Spirit tugs at your heart, please respond to Him. Protection is not only for you but for others who the enemy is trying to connect to you. Six years of being infected with the toxic waste from not being healed from relationships. SIX YEARS of my life I will never get back. We never got back to the "healthy" place in our relationship. I know now that this was God trying to protect me from this relationship because He is all about relationships! He was born, lived, and died just to pursue your heart and have an intimate relationship with you. However, He does not want you in the WRONG one. After being sick from such an emotional rollercoaster ride, I made the hardest decision in my life; I took a trip to the clinic. My womb, a place that was designed for comfort, peace, and life, became a dark, dismal tomb for the life that was growing on the inside of me. I remember telling God, if you want me to come walk away from this healed and free, you are going to literally have to do all of the walking and freeing because I am done with life. I am done with people. I am done with myself. Here I am, in my right mind, free, whole, forgiven and HEALED. Through six years of pain and hardships, God stayed by my side! He gave me beauty for ashes! He never left me! He gave me a new life; even after I ended one and took my own for granted. GOD WAS THERE!

After the Amen

All the single ladies, all the single ladies!! How many of you can relate to one of the Beyoncé's hottest tunes? I can! As I stated earlier, I thought that I would be married by now but I am not, at least not to a real man. The bible does tell us that we are already married! We have a heavenly bridegroom and His name is Jesus Christ! If you are like me, you have thought when is God is going to send my "Boaz." When is my knight in shining armor going to come and rescue me from the dragons of singleness? When am I going to be able to announce to the world that I am finally off of the market? During my singleness, I have discovered a profound truth: falling ever so sweetly in love with Jesus Christ will remove your heart out of any ditch of discontentment that it may have driven you into during your journey of singleness. Surrendering to our heavenly Father of wanting life to happen on our terms is one of the most liberating feelings that you will ever experience. I have found myself so many times expecting God to provide the blessing after my "amen". Lord, please bless me with this,

Lord, please bless with me that. Lord, please bless me with a husband. Amen. And nothing happens. There is no cloud coming from the ceiling with my Boaz. Situations are not instantly changed. I am still driving the same car. I am still single. We do know that the God we serve is sovereign and powerful and if He wanted too, He could instantly, quicker than we can think, perform those miracles and provide us, with the desires of our heart. But the picture is bigger than that. He wants our WHOLE heart, not just our wants and wishes! As singles, God wants us to trust Him with our plans and believe that He knows the who, what, when, and where of the things that He has in store for us. This is the place for God to receive the best from us. Time to serve others, connect with the right people, accomplish goals, and not be distracted with the cares and responsibilities that a husband and family will bring. God knows what you desire. He even knows things to bless you with that you don't even know to ask for! That's power! *I knew you before I formed you in your mother's womb. Before you were born I set you apart and appointed you as my prophet to the nations." Jeremiah 1:5.* Every intricate detail, every intimate demand, He knows about you. He wants to meet you where you are, establish an intimate relationship with you, heal your heart, love you more than you or anyone else can love you, and hold you at night when you feel lonely on yet another dateless Friday night. If singles can understand that God has so much in store for us during this time, it will lift the "weight" from us while we "wait" during this season. Understand that God is willing to bless you after your "amen" but you have to be ready to work and wait for it. There is work required in waiting for what God has for you. Not necessarily physical work, but strength to endure, patience, believing, and trusting that He is going to bring everything to pass. I will be the first to say that it is definitely easier said than done but, with anything that you want, you work hard for. The best miracles take time. The same is true while you are trusting God for a mate. Work on becoming the best that you can be so that you can be an asset and not a liability to your spouse! Be patient in God's timing and believe that He hears your prayers and release your total faith after your "amen". When you relinquish the right of wanting life on your terms, you will experience God's faithfulness in your life. Often times, the Holy Spirit reminds me that God does not need my help in making things happen. I don't have to manipulate situations to get them to work in my favor. If God wants us to experience a situation, meet the right person, He WILL make it happen in His own way and time. We don't have to maneuver to try and get what we want. We can trust the Creator of all mankind to blow our minds and bless us with the things we desire. God has a proven track record of getting people together. If you need a reminder, please read one of the most incredible love stories in the bible, the book of Ruth. Oftentimes we get so caught up on the fact that Boaz was this great individual that we miss the entire message of the book. Ruth was patient and obedient to God! It was her reckless abandonment to everything that she knew, her ways of life, and her family. Ruth obeyed God and followed her mother- in- law to her home and served! Because of her obedience, God was faithful and rewarded her obedience and patience with Boaz, whose name means "pillar of strength." If God can bless Ruth in a foreign land where there was no potential mate in sight, he will surely bless you in your "foreign" place, your singleness if you remain faithful. God knew all along that Ruth would meet Boaz. It is when we are willing to surrender our life, trust God and step into the unknown of our faith that God will bless us with "a pillar of strength." If you are in an extended season of singleness, do not question where God is at this point. Whether it has been days, months, or even years, God has a plan with you in mind. He has not forgotten about you. I have discovered that God will extend our season of singleness, not because we have more to work on, but to give our future mate time to become the person they need to be for you. A lot of singles think that they are doomed for a lifetime of singleness because the wait has become longer than they anticipated. God may be using this extra time to "perfect" your Boaz or Ruth. Trust God. Pray for your future spouse during this time. Lift them up in your daily prayer time with the Lord. Ask God for more opportunities to serve others or help you in areas that you lack so that you enter into the marriage relationship whole! And at the right time, on the right day, God will reveal his favor to you by introducing you to your future spouse. He is here, Right now, writing your love story! How marvelous it will be.

The Conversation in the Waiting Room

Until recently, I have had the pleasure of having both of my biological grandmothers in my life. Their presence in my life has been beneficial not only to my academic success, but to my overall well-being as a young woman. August 16, 2013, my grandmother Katherine Jones passed away. A small, but mighty and powerful woman! She was always about her business and she ALWAYS meant business. August 16th will never be the same for me. There is a void from her absence in my life. The memories, home cooked meals, stories of my aunts and uncles and mother when they were children, the water jug she would put outside for my cousins and me when we were children growing up because we couldn't come in the house once we were outside unless it was for a drastic reason. Her countless jokes that she would always make. Her sayings to certain situations in life, which were hilarious and sometimes inappropriate. Her smile at all three of my college graduations. There are so many things that I could mention that I am going to miss about her, but for twenty seven years of my life, I was able to be around, laugh, talk, cry, and tell her any and everything that was going on in my life. She was a mother to many and the relationship that we shared will always remain with me. Rest well Mama!

Ruthie Gaines, "my granny" as I call her is the mother of my father. I am her only grandchild and she loves me more than life itself. One of the most amazing things that I absolutely love about both of my grandmothers is that they had a relationship with each other! I love the way that they talked, called each other on occasions, sent each other meals, gave me tough love when I needed it, and both called me on my work phone instead of my cell phone when they needed me. My granny is probably the only person in my entire life that never told me no. There was a time when I was younger and I almost burned her house down. There was a cigarette lighter on the table and I got curious. I lit the napkin that my daily snack was wrapped in and dropped it on the floor when the fire started to burn my hand. My grandmother put the fire out with her foot and asked me what happened. Of course I didn't do it, so I blamed it on my friend down the street! {Laughing out loud right now}. She spanked me and then cried because she had to do that!

Really? If I was her, I would spank my grandchild every time I thought about the situation! But because of the love that she has for me, it hurt her to have to discipline me. I deserved it and she never had to do it again. There is probably nothing that I could think of that I want or need that my grandmother would not provide. Inspite of all of the material things, my grandmother and I had a conversation that is priceless and is far more precious than anything tangible. When my grandmother and I had this conversation, she did not know that I was going through a really bad time in my relationship. She would always ask me "So Nisi, where is your boyfriend" and on this day I was really going through it with my ex-boyfriend. Our relationship was over but we were in that dumb awkward phase of trying to fix a broken relationship that was in a million pieces of the "why her", "so this is what that meant", "that's why you couldn't answer the phone", "that's where you were", etc. Trying to put back together a broken relationship only left me cut and hurt from the pain I inflicted myself with of "trying to work it out." I told her that I was single and she said good! I was confused because she had just asked me where my boyfriend was. She said stay that way until you know. Until I know what? Until you know when it's right. "When I was your age, I had two kids and I was married to a man who was a drunk. Countless of times I hid the pain from physical and verbal abuse that he inflicted upon me. I always held it inside and never talked about it. At this point, my eyes were filled with tears because I couldn't believe that this happened to my granny! She is the sweetest lady on the planet! I asked her what advice you would give me at this point in my life being a young single Christian woman. She said "wait!" Don't rush! You have plenty of time to get married and have children. Enjoy your life. Do things that you want to do now because when you are married with a family; it is no longer about you but the cares and concerns of your family. She said when I finally started to talk about what was going on at home with me and your Papa, I felt better. When you are hurting, don't hold it in. Let it out. You will feel better. As much as I love your aunt and dad, I wish I would have waited. My mind was blown! My granny loves her children and her life, but to know the things that she was going through when she was my age is humbling. I know you are probably thinking that there is nothing unusual about this conversation, but it is. What I have discovered is that as young single women, we don't have enough older women telling us to wait! And not just to wait idly, but to wait on God with an expectancy that He is going to do just what He said. In a culture where women have dominated the charts in their careers and personal successes, life, love, and REALNESS isn't discussed. I have a lot of successful, boss lady "swagged out" single and female LONLEY friends. There is absolutely nothing wrong with pursuing your dreams and establishing a comfortable lifestyle for yourself. I also know that not every woman desires to get married and have children. However, if all you have to offer to the world are your degrees, status, and bank account, you really don't have much to offer and not worth much. I am not saying that what you have accomplished isn't to be commended or applauded; however, being a woman of substance, experience and truth will take your further in life than any piece of paper. A lot of young people get so caught up in making a living that we forget to make and enjoy life. Tangible things are of value for so long. 2 Corinthians 4:18 clearly tells us *"as we look not to the things that are seen but to the things that are unseen. For the things that are seen are transient, but the things that are unseen are eternal.'"* The bible teaches us that only what we do for Christ for last! Our daily "grinding" should only be a small percentage of what we have to offer to the generations to come. As young successful Christian women, we should have more to give back to the younger women than just our status. I am not sure about you, but my road to success was not a straight, smooth, narrow one. Life happened to me. I struggled. Times were hard. I made mistakes. I missed the mark. I experienced some low and dark places, all while on the road to becoming successful. That's why I do not mind sharing my testimony with any young woman or anyone in general because you never know how you being real, open, and honest can help them in their life. This is why the conversation that my grandmother and I had means so much to me because she was able to nurture my spirit. She gave me something that neither three of my degrees will ever be able to give me; Godly wisdom. She told me the truth. Regardless of how successful I am, I can't minister and help save souls with my degrees. But I can tell how my dark and difficult times are a part of my destiny and have made me determined to become all that God is calling me to be. I am able to take the precious advice that she gave me and not only apply it to my life, but I can use it to minister to another sister who may need it as well. One thing that I have learned about life is that the "waiting room" is a place that everyone must go at some point. In order to build healthy strong muscles physically, there has to be some weightlift training. If you want to have strong abs, solid quads, and a firm gluteus maximums, some weight and resistance training has to take place. The same is required when you are in the waiting room of life! While you are in the "waiting room" this is an opportunity to build strong muscles of faith and patience. *Isaiah 40:31 says "Yet those who wait on the Lord will gain a new strength; they will mount up with wings like eagles, they will run and not get tired, they will walk and not become weary."* Without the weight training in the "wait" room, you will leave the situations of life the same way you came in. Your mindset has to be positive while training. You will not see instant results, but with persistence, consistency, and endurance, things will begin to change. You will begin to run faster, lift heavier weights, become stronger, and walk and not become weary. When you wait on the Lord, and you pour your entire self into the "training" you will notice that your faith has increased, past hurts are healed places in your life, things that were designed to destroy you are now shaping you for your destiny, people who you never received an apology from are forgiven! Another element that is vital to a success weight training class is REST. In your "waiting" season, your singleness, God will give you rest to endure the wait! Hallelujah! What an awesome God we serve. Rest is vital to your time in the "waiting" room. God calls us to rest in Him. God is calling you to do great things in your "waiting" season, but if you aren't well rested, you will not have the energy to successfully complete the task! Your body and mind has to experience rest after a vigorous weight training session in order to continue the training! You need to rest after a divorce. You need to rest after your heart has been broken. You need to rest after the loss of a loved one. You need to rest after a broken relationship or engagement. You need to rest after the physical and verbal abuse. You need to rest after the unacceptable lifestyle. You need to rest after being addicted to drugs and alcohol. You need to rest after you ended a pregnancy. There is healing in your resting place. There is deliverance in your resting place. There is understanding in your resting place. There is peace is your resting place. There is wholeness in your resting place. There is patience in your resting place. While in the "waiting" room of your singleness, rest in God's promises to you! And after you are strong, healthy, and whole, God will deliver you from your waiting into what He has in store for you.

Old Hymn

Summertime in the country at my grandmother's house was always my favorite time. I don't have siblings so my cousins and I would spend all day playing, plotting, and having fun with one another. My grandmother would cook us hot cooked meals every day, snacks to keep us sustained and her infamous water jug would be set outside for my cousins and me to drink out of all throughout the day because she wouldn't let us come in and out of the house. Only for drastic reasons, such as using the bathroom or if we had an emergency, and that was according to her definition of what an emergency was. When I was younger, I thought that she was just a tad bit extreme because of her rules for my cousins and me during the summer, but looking back, I understand why she reared us the way that she did. We learned how to survive individually and collectively. We bonded. We looked after one another. We argued. We made up. We played together. We caught lightening bugs, grasshoppers, played football; we made cars out of fold up chairs and used old hubcaps as the driving wheel. We created games;

we walked to the local store, which was the highlight of our day sometimes. Four square became one of our favorite games and sometimes for old times' sake, we still play when we are all together. There are so many memories that I have from growing up in the country with my cousins. Because of all the time that we spent together, we are all still really close. We ALL love to sit outside because we spent a lot of our childhood out there! It's a place that we all can talk about and relate to because of the time we spent growing up as kids together. On the inside of the house, along with my grandmother and her strict rules and her extra clean baseboards was my great grandmother, Mattie Mae Hall. She was the rock, the matriarch, the QUEEN of our family. She was a feisty, head strong, strong woman. Even in her old age, she was a woman of influence and dignity! Every day she would call me or another one of my girl cousins to come into the house and rub her feet, scratch her back, or scratch her head and braid her hair. When the time came each day for one of us to do it, we would sometimes roll our eyes, talk underneath our breath, or just have an attitude because we knew that no matter how hard we tried, she was going to tell us that we were doing it wrong...LOL. While we were being her masseuse, she would make us say the Lord's Prayer, our timetables, and certain scriptures that she taught us. You always wanted to make sure that you knew those things, because you were going to be tested! If you didn't know them or if you messed up from being nervous in front of her, you would have a headache for days because she would ball up her fist and bang us in the forehead! And then she would say "If you don't learn the Lord's Prayer, I am going to knock you to Polio." My cousins and I still have no earthly idea what or where Polio is until this day, however, I am sure some of us wanted to go there instead of being beat in the forehead with knuckles and gold rings. While we were doing our assigned duties, my grandmother would sing. We would all look at each other and giggle because she was not quite the vocalist. She would sing old hymns that I didn't understand. I understood the words but I didn't comprehend the meaning and message of the song. While she sung, we couldn't talk. If I was scratching her head and braiding her hair, she would say "don't talk over me" if my cousin was rubbing her feet, she couldn't say anything. All we could do is listen to her sing these hymns that we didn't know or like! It wasn't until I got older and started to experience life for myself that I actually begin to understand what happened at that time in my life with my great grandmother. I didn't know that at the time when my great grandmother would sing her hymns that she was really planting a seed in me that I would need to use its fruit from later on in my life. She would cry and begin to praise God while she was singing these old songs and I didn't understand why she was so emotional. My cousins and I were so confused and stayed quiet until she finished. It was just an old song that we sung at church out of the red hymn books that were on the back of each pew. What was so powerful about these songs that made her cry and praise God the way she did when she sung them? Sometimes she wouldn't even be able to finish the song before she started to worship God through her tears. There was a time in my life where I was so broken. My heart was broken, my spirit was broken, and my soul was broken. It was at that moment that I heard my great grandmothers' voice singing the old hymn. I heard her voice in my mind so clearly singing "Father, I stretch my hands to Thee, No other help I know; if thou withdraw thyself from me, whither shall I go?"

When I was a young girl scratching and braiding my grandmother's hair and she would say "don't talk over me" I couldn't understand why she would say that. My mind and spirit needed to be quiet so that those words could deposit deep down in my soul so that later on in my broken moments, I would be able to use the fruit that it produced from those seeds that she planted in me over the years from being rooted so deep! Woo!! I know now that she wasn't being mean but she was sending me a message that I would use later on in my life. In my broken moments, in my disappointing moments, in my setbacks, in my mistakes, in my failures, I can sing the old hymn that my grandmother used to sing and say "Father, I stretch my hands to Thee!" I understand why she would cry and praise God while singing that hymn because she would think about the things that she had gone through and that she was still here to pour into all of us so that later on in our lives when she wasn't around to sing to us, we could sing and encourage ourselves! Now I understand why my grandmother wasn't able to finish the song sometimes because now I don't even have to sing the song; I can think about the words in the song and begin to praise

God because I understand the message. They aren't just words from a red book that sit on the back of pews; it is a prescription for my ailing spirit and soul for me to meditate on in times of distress and discontentment. This song is not just my great grandmothers' testimony but I am a living witness of it myself and can testify that there is No other Help I know! "Father, I stretch my hands to Thee" in my times of trouble and pain! "No other help I know" when my friends and family can't be found and I have ran out of resources of trying to do things my way. "If Thou withdraw Thyself from me" after I have sinned time and time again, after I have neglected your love and guidance, and after I have taken for granted your grace, "whither shall I go?" after I have tried the ways of the world over and over, after I have purposely made the decisions that I have made. Lord thank you for being a present help and because of your selfless act of love on Calvary, I can stretch my hands to Thee! The words of this hymn does something to my soul when I think about or sing the song. My great grandmother understood for herself, and now I understand for myself and I am thankful that she was not ashamed to let us know what God had done for her. I have experienced enough of life to understand the power in this song. I know that I can stretch my hands anytime, anywhere, at any moment that I might need my Father. Ladies, during your singleness, allow this hymn to minister to your heart. Stretch your hands towards heaven and surrender anything that may be weighing you down. Understand that you can stretch your hands and allow God to calm your restlessness and the torture of desire during this season. Use this hymn and this time to thank God from protecting you from harmful, unproductive relationships that you could have been in. Thank Him for not withdrawing Himself from you right now. Thank Him for being that Help that is like none other. I am thankful for the wisdom that my great grandmother shared with me. Even though I had to experience life for myself and I had to go through some difficult times, because of what was put on the inside of me, I was able to endure and overcome those obstacles. As a young single woman who has had her heart broken more than once, to have that wisdom deposited into my spirit at such a young age has given me exactly what I needed to allow my brokenness to heal. I know the Healer because of my great grandmother so that in my trying times, the old hymn that she sung would give me new life and meaning and soothe my soul with ease. Regardless of the situation that you may be in or coming out of, sing the words of the hymn and allow God to give you what you need at this moment in your life.

The Tin Building

I found out I was pregnant a month before I was about to graduate from college with my Bachelor's Degree. I really didn't have any symptoms and I still had my menstrual cycle so I didn't think of anything being wrong. Slight cravings, headaches more than normal, but nothing was out of the ordinary. Two months into my pregnancy is when the doctors told me that I was with child. I was confused, shocked, embarrassed and devastated because my boyfriend and I officially broke up the week before after a huge fight that consisted of me breaking his windows with a candle and destroying anything else that I could get my hands on during one of the most dangerous fights that we had. The look on my mother's face broke my already shattered heart into a million more pieces when I told her that I was pregnant. She always told me that she wanted me to finish college, explore the world, and do things the right way when it came to children and marriage. Even though I was getting ready to walk across the stage the very next month, I felt like the biggest failure. After hearing the ultra sound and seeing my baby, the doctor informed me that my baby's heartbeat was slow. This was typical in the early stages but I was almost three months. I begin to experience bleeding and rushed myself to the hospital. Stress, disappointment, confusion, hatred, brokenness, all began to take a toll on my mind, body, and my unborn. So many thoughts went through my mind. I had so many emotions, that I really couldn't focus on anything. Why me? Out of all of the times that we had sex, unprotected, why would I get pregnant now? My boyfriend and I were not on speaking terms, and all I could think in my mind was "Me? This is happening to me?" I was by no means perfect nor did I think I was, but I never thought that this would happen to me. Pregnant! Something I said I would wait for marriage for. I always wanted my children to live in the same household as both of their biological parents because I never received the opportunity. I wanted better for my children and future. What was I going to do with a baby? What could I give my baby? A baby?! I cried tears of joy and sadness at the same time. To some extent I was excited that there was life growing on the inside of me and then on the other hand, I was terrified and disappointed with myself. I contemplated long and hard about this situation. I have never felt so many emotions going on within me at the same time. I couldn't focus. I couldn't eat. I couldn't sleep. I couldn't do anything because I didn't know what to do. I found myself becoming depressed because I had no control over my emotions or being pregnant. What would my family think? What would my friends think? What would God think of me? I am not married. This relationship that God told me not to get in is over. How do I be a mother? Where would I work? I couldn't turn my brain off! I began to consider other options. I found an abortion clinic that would end the pregnancy. Did I really want to do this? Did I really just Google this? Abortion was something I said that I would never do. Would my baby survive anyway due to the slow heartbeat, constant headaches, and physical stress that I was experiencing? The doctor said it was a 50/50 chance and that they had seen both happen. I called the clinic and made an appointment. Immediately the enemy began to tell me how horrible of a person I was and that I was stupid. Satan began to toy with my mind. He told me I was worthless, a murderer, not good enough, and other negative demonic thoughts. I had so much going through my mind. I began to think about all of the times that I could have left this relationship and moved forward with my life. Why didn't I leave after certain situations? As I reflect back on those times and situations, and how I decided to pursue my will instead of God's and how I tried to fix all of my problems with sex, it dawned on me how much power it had in my life. It began to make sense as to why I couldn't leave my relationship because I was tied to it. And not just any tie. But an unholy soul tie! A soul tie that kept me in bondage. An unholy soul tie that served as a bridge to pass demonic garbage!! I was connected to mess! To trash! To ungodliness! And because I was connected to those things, I found myself at an abortion clinic. Life is all about choices. You can choose the sin, but you can't choose the consequence. God never intended me to be connected to those things and He never intended for me to end up at that place, but I chose what I wanted to do and not what He was calling to me to do. This experience has made me very cautious about relationships and friendships that I enter into now because the devil desires to tie you to things and people that are poison and I encourage you to be cautious as well. Don't just enter into relationships or friendships because you miss the human touch or the presence of someone being in your life. Strengthen your relationship with Jesus before you stress yourself out about being with someone who He never intended you to be with from the beginning. If your relationship with Christ is solid, He will allow the right people to come into your life that will only take you to higher heights, encourage you to become better, and remain consistent regardless of what life brings. It all looked good and sounded good and felt good while I was in that relationship, but when I found myself at this place, NONE of that was ever any good! There were times when the enemy would heavily pursue my mind, thoughts, and dreams with the decision that I made. I tried to "just forget about it". That didn't work. It wasn't until I ran out of myself, my opinions, my ways of dealing with the situation that the healing began. I had to take all of it to Jesus. It was hard. It was a long tough process, but God had to heal EVERY broken piece that I had. It took months and years for me to even talk about and tell the truth about my experience. It was then that I started to feel a weight of shame and guilt lifted from me. Even though that was a dark place in my life, the light of Christ now shines bright in my life. I remember having nightmares about it and waking up out of my sleep. I remember crying so hard on the due date that I couldn't go to work or really function that day. But after I took it to Jesus and prayed and received forgiveness and forgave myself, I now know now that I had an authentic encounter with Jesus. When you totally surrender any experience or yourself to Jesus, the blood will wash away any sin or inequities that the devil tries to keep you in bondage with. Regardless of where you are in your life and situations that you have ended, whether it is a toxic relationship, an engagement or a friendship be encouraged because, there is a light that will lead you out of it. My womb, a place of comfort and protection became a dark tomb for my unborn. Allow God to use your times of darkness and make them work out for your destiny! Give God all of the pieces and allow Him to give you the wisdom and grace within so that you can birth goals, dreams and ambitions. God can and will resurrect and restore dark places in your life and give you beauty for your ashes! Some young woman needs to know there is forgiveness and healing even after you have made the decision to end a pregnancy. Ending the pregnancy is only the beginning. This decision is not a "cure all" to live a normal life after an unplanned pregnancy. Your life doesn't go back to normal nor is there a sense of relief. It hurt. Really bad. After many times of thinking about ending my life because I chose to end the life of my unborn, I knew that I needed to have an encounter with the comforter. There is a long road of recovery ahead of you. One of the many lessons that I learned throughout all of this is pursuit. I had to pursue healing. I had to pursue peace of mind, pursue Christ. Putting the same amount of energy, time, effort and heart into Him, the way I did my relationship, things and people. If I would have given my ENTIRE self to my relationship with Christ, I wouldn't have found myself in this situation. I encourage you to examine the relationships that you are currently in. Seek God for answers about your significant other. Don't ignore the tug and pull at your heart from the Holy Spirit. If you have found yourself in this situation and these relationships, learn from your experiences. I encourage you lady to give all of the pieces to Christ. Allow Him to forgive you and give you the strength that you need to pursue Him passionately. If you have been holding on to guilt and shame because of the decision that you have made, stop reading right now and cry out to God. If you are contemplating this decision, please understand that there is a better way! Though it may seem like the quickest way for this to all be over, it actually all starts once it's over! Pain, regret, shame, and guilt are only a few of the many emotions that you will experience. It's not an easy decision. It's not a "cure all" to an unplanned pregnancy. God instructs us to choose life! In every area of our lives! This was a hard situation for me to deal with. I cried a lot, and often. I felt empty. One of the most profound moments that I can recall about this situation is the pregnancy care center in Stephenville, Texas where I was living at the time. I went to the center to have an ultrasound, receive pregnancy care, and information on what was going on with my body. Before I left the center one of the ladies called me into a private room and asked me some personal questions about my relationship with my boyfriend and she asked me if I knew Jesus. I told her yes. She embraced me and prayed with me and looked me in the face and spoke peace and blessings over my life. She never judged me because I told her I wasn't sure what I was going to do about everything. She told me that she understood and then she grabbed my hand and offered me Jesus.

So now I offer you Jesus! He's such a gentleman! Ask for forgiveness, peace, and wisdom and begin to walk in it. Pray for release, refreshment, and renewing of your mind and body! Meditate on Hebrews 8:12 *"For I will be merciful to their iniquities, and I will remember their sins no more."* Let go! Get up! That abortion is not who you are, God has so much more for you. Learn from this experience and allow it to position yourself for things greater to come. Allow this experience to drive you to strive harder. Set goals and work hard to accomplish them. Allow God full access in all areas of your life. After I ended my pregnancy, over time, many prayers, sleepless nights, crying often, reflecting back on my past and seeking God for direction, I began to feel better. Day by day the weight of guilt and shame began to come off of me. I went back to school and finished my Master's Degree in a 1 ½. I was determined that I would not feel sorry for myself but instead, use this situation for God to set me up for success, and He has done just that. I am able to talk about my experience and allow God to use my story to encourage you and others who may have or may be going through the same. I am a firm believer of learning lessons without having to encounter the actual experience. Learn from others who have gone through things. Embrace my story so that it won't become yours. No longer do I feel ashamed or embarrassed about my experience because God doesn't see me that way. There are some who know about this and there are others who don't but when you look at me, I can guarantee you that I don't look like what I have been through! That statement isn't coming from a conceited place, because I will not and cannot ever take the credit for the young lady that I am today. Wisdom came from my wounds. I had to lie on my face plenty of times and cry out to God so that I could be free. God is ready to do the same for you. God has forgiven me and equipped me to share my story with the expectation of inspiring and encouraging others. If more women would be willing to be open and honest and share with their sisters the things that God has brought them out of and saved them from, an entire generational shift would take place. More women would feel compelled to run to Jesus, throw themselves at His feet, receive His forgiveness and love and go out and tell the world what the Savior has done for them. Some young Christian, successful, attractive woman is waiting to hear that someone else has gone through the exact same thing that she is going through right now or has gone through but hasn't dealt with. Well this chapter is for you. Cry out to Jesus! Take your best and your broken, your alabaster box and break it at His feet. He is waiting for you! Be free beautiful lady! God STILL has more for you! Don't allow your past or people to postpone the purpose and plans that are in place for you. Stand tall. Be bold and declare that Jesus is Lord and by the blood that was selflessly shed on Calvary; you are healed, set free, and redeemed.

Not Enough

After everything that I had gone through with my mom, relationship, and ending my pregnancy, I still had moments where I felt like I wasn't enough and nothing I did was enough. I graduated with my Bachelor's Degree, started my career, and had gotten accepted into the Master's Degree Program, but I just felt as if something was missing. I didn't understand what was wrong with me because I had positive things going for myself. I discovered that I still had some broken parts that hadn't fully healed yet. Broken views of myself. Things that I had to go through that I didn't think that I would or did I plan for. Little small pieces of insecurities, trust issues with people, just little things that I knew if weren't healed soon would become big issues later on in life. In John chapter 6, the bible tells us the story when Jesus fed five thousand people. One of His disciples asked Him where are we going to get enough food to feed these people. Even though the disciple couldn't figure out how this miracle was going to take place, Jesus already had a plan in mind! I have learned that even when situations look impossible and at the time when I felt like I wasn't enough, God already had a plan in mind for me. Unlike the disciple, we as believers need to pass the test of faith and know that God is everything that we need Him to be and that any need we have, He can and will supply when situations around us seem impossible. When Andrew, another one of Jesus's disciples saw a young boy with five small barley loaves and two small fish, he requested that Jesus used that to feed the masses, but his faith still wavered while in the presence of the Master. Jesus gave the disciples instructions to assemble the people so that he could perform one of the most incredible miracles in the bible. *"Jesus then took the loaves, blessed it and then broke it to distribute to the people."* The blessing was in the breaking! After Jesus broke the bread, two fish and five loads fed five thousand! Only an all knowing, sovereign, powerful Master can perform such a miracle in breaking! It was in my brokenness that God was giving me instructions to position myself so that He could bless me. I didn't understand it at the time. I felt like God had abandoned me and that I was being punished for some of the things that I had done. I didn't realize that that was the place, my brokenness, God was actually blessing me! It didn't feel good nor did it look good because when something breaks, pain is normally the result. I remember breaking one of my mother's china dishes and trying to hide it from her only to discover that some of the pieces fell on the kitchen floor and she stepped on it and realized that it was her broken china. The very same mistake that I tried to hide left residue that I didn't realize, and she ended stepping on one of the pieces. Don't try and hide any pieces from God. He knows about them anyway! Take them all to Him! Allow God to use every broken piece of your life so that when He is finished repairing you, you will be able to bless others with all of the pieces that you thought God couldn't use. After having gone through so much and not feeling good enough, God took all of those broken pieces, blessed me, and now is using my testimony to feed and minister the word of God to the masses! If God can use two fish and five loaves of bread to get glory, imagine what He can and will do with your brokenness. If I had not surrendered all of my pieces, I would not be the young lady that I am today. No longer do I worry when things get hard for me because all I do is reflect back on a time when I felt so low, hurt, empty, and broken and I am reminded of the miracle that God performed then. I have gotten to the point to where I don't have to depend on finding out who God is from others, because I know Him all too well for myself. As a young woman, having a personal, intimate relationship with Christ has allowed me to use everything that I have gone through and wait patiently on God. I want to do things the right way. I want to avoid heartbreak from people who God never intended me to receive it from. I want to avoid discontentment and instead discover the mystery of contentment. I don't want any broken pieces of my past to get in the way of the plan and purpose that God has for me. Young lady, take all of your pieces to God and leave them there and when He is finished putting you back together again, you my sister will also have a story to tell the world!

This Place

At the beginning of the book, I told you that I thought I had it all figured out. It's the end of the book, and I have something else to tell you; I don't! And I am fine with that. I never would have thought that I would have gone through some of the things that I did, but as I look back in retrospect I have a greater appreciation for those things that I had to endure. Romans 8:28 tells us that ALL of those things worked together for my good. That might sound crazy, but it is the truth. If everything that happened to me didn't happen to me, I wouldn't be in THIS place. That's not to say that I wouldn't still be in a good place in my life, but it wouldn't be this one! This place is a place of peace. A place of wholeness. A place of gratefulness. A place of redemption. A place of forgiveness. A place of rest and restoration. At 28 years of age, I am experiencing the ultimate peace of God. I have learned lessons and encountered situations and experiences that people older in age would never imagine. I am glad that I am at a place at a young age to where I have learned so much now so as I get older and continue to experience life's challenges, I have previous lessons to reflect upon. I do not want to be in my 40's married with children trying to learn how to trust God. This place of singleness, undistracted and trusted time from the Lord is serving as my classroom for this. Ladies, your singleness is a gift from God because He is giving you time to search His heart and devote yourself, time and energy into kingdom building. This is a place and time for you to become your best self. This is a place and time for you to have reckless abandonment for Christ. Make you happy! Get back to yourself. Set goals and accomplish them. Get out of debt. Travel the world. Spend time with family. Serve in ministry at your church. In this place, I am discovering the mystery of contentment. In the bible, the apostle Paul gives clear instructions on contentment." *I know what it is to be in need, and I know what it is to have plenty. I have learned the secret of being content in any and every situation, whether well fed or hungry, whether living in plenty or in want." Philippians 4:11* Ladies, we know all too well about secrets! A secret is something that we all have discussed with our closest friends. This amazing man of God is giving us a secret that will not only help us in this place of singleness, but in every other area of our lives as well! The apostle was in jail when he decided to share his secret with us. He not only shared his secret with us, but this is a challenge for us as well. While in your "jail of singleness", are you willing to be content and are you willing to share this secret with other women? Are you willing to take all of your desires to Jesus and rest in this place in your life? Are you ready to stop trying to manipulate and maneuver situations so that you can get what you think you want in this place in your life? God is ready to use you exactly in the place that you are in your life. God is giving you the best of Himself in this place in your life! It's just you and him darling! You have His undivided attention, and now it's time for you to stop pouting and give Him yours. In this place, some days are easier than others when the desire to have a mate comes upon me. But, in this same place God quiets the torture of desire and replaces it with thirst and hunger for His word to be better, know better and do better so that when He sends the man that He created just for me, it is in this place that I move from preparation to promise! This is the place that God knew I would need after all of the things that I went through. A place where His voice is so clear and His presence is ever present. Tamela Mann has a song on her cd that is titled "This Place" and in the song she is singing to her listeners that she never thought that she would be in a place of freedom and peace and to be able to live beyond her past. This is one of my favorite songs because I can relate to every verse and word that she sings. The vamp to the song says *"Oh I'm glad I'm living my life in this place"* I am not sure about you, but I am glad that I am living my life in this place! After seeing my mother face death, I am glad that I am living in this place to see her face every day and to witness the healing power of Jesus. After being heartbroken, lied too, cheated on, taken for granted, I am glad that I am living my life in this place of wholeness, healing, and freedom. After ending a pregnancy and almost losing my mind and being broken over something that was designed to destroy me, I am glad that I am living in this place of forgiveness, redemption, grace and mercy! I am so glad for this place! This place is divine! This is the place where God is! He was there in all of this! Invite Him to your place! Be blessed my sister!

From My heart to Yours

I have always known that I have had the "gift of gab" but I never thought that I would write a book. I wanted to share my heart and life with you in hopes that you or maybe someone you know will be inspired and encouraged. Being a part of the younger generation, I have realized that a lot of us are hurting. We are a hurting and angry generation. We have had to endure things and situations and grow up before we wanted too and the result of those experiences has left us emotionally torn, scared, and abused. I wanted to share my story with you so that you know that you are not alone. You aren't the only person who has been heartbroken by the one person you trusted so much of yourself with. You aren't the only person who has experienced an unplanned pregnancy and then ended the life. You aren't the only beautiful, successful young woman who has felt empty and contemplated suicide. I was that woman. I experienced those things as well. I felt worthless and ashamed too. When I think about all of those feelings and negative emotions that I experienced, I come to the realization that I am not the only person who has gone through these things. In the bible, it tells a story of a woman who was caught in the act of adultery. Everyone wanted to kill her by throwing stones at her because of the things that she had done. The ironic and phenomenal part of the story was that the only person present that day that COULD have stoned her and was actually without sin, didn't! That is the beauty and epitome of grace! God knows what we deserve when we miss the mark.

He knows that when we are disobedient to his word that our consequences SHOULD be death, but that would defeat the purpose of Calvary. The grace of God will show up and fight for you. Everyone present that day were sinners themselves. But when you have established a right relationship with God and you have surrendered your life, those same sinners who tried to put your business on blast and make you feel like you are not worthy, will have to drop their stones and walk away because grace is on your side. God knew that without His son, humanity wouldn't last long on earth. So my point is this: When people try to "stone" you for your mistakes or when you try to stone yourself, take pleasure in knowing that grace will speak up for you. All of us has sinned. We have all missed the mark. We have all made mistakes. Don't allow the opinions of others to shame you or make you feel less than. Receive God's grace and forgiveness because there will come a time when you will have to share your heart and experiences with someone else and you won't be able to do that if you are worried about what other sinners are going to say. Your life is your message to the world. Make sure that it is inspiring. My heart is for you. My heart loves you. My heart pleads and prays for you. This is my heart to you.

"The most beautiful people we have known are those who have known defeat, known suffering, known struggle, known loss, and have found their way out of the depths. These persons have an appreciation, sensitivity, and an understanding of life that fills them with compassion, gentleness, and a deep loving concern. Beautiful people do not just happen."

~ Elisabeth Kübler-Ross

Conclusion

This book is a rare purpose driven treasure of Godly wisdom, totally scriptural, inspired by the spirit, and born of life experience and insight. God has used Shaniece as an effective instrument, and this book revels why. She's kept grounded on eternal values and rooted in the vine of the ultimate truth "Christ Jesus". These life experiences will revolutionize and energize anyone to reach their full potential. Fifty years from now young and old adults will have this book on their shelf beside their bible. It will last for generations to come for its teachings and principles are timeless, for its hard to argue with biblical principles and the voice of experience.

"Psalm 145:4 teaches us that one generation will commend your works to another; they will tell of your mighty acts." "Acts 13:36, tells us that David was purpose driven: when David had served God's purpose in his own generation, he [died]."

I cannot think of a greater epitaph. Imagine having that statement inscribed on your tombstone: "he served God's purpose in his own generation". The fact is we can't serve God in any other generation except our own. Ministry must always be done in the context of the current generation and culture. We must minister to people in the culture as it really is -- not in some past form that we may have idealized in our minds. This book is relevant, timely, biblical and contemporary without compromising the truth, while inspiring a generation. In every era, God raises up leaders to pioneer new possibilities for that generation of His people. God gave Shaniece the gift of vision and discernment, and the results can be seen in the writings of this novel, for it is the authentic blueprint of the 21st century generation and contains as much proven growth wisdom as any book ever written from life experience. "Psalms 35:27 says praise the greatness of The Lord, who loves to see His servants do well." If you want to dream great dreams, grow a healthier you, and accomplish God's purpose in your generation, this book is for you. My prayer is that everyone that read this book, believes it, be prepared to stand corrected by it, and change to match its sound scriptural wisdom. On a Sunday at 10:18 am September 29, 1985 the world was introduced to

Shaniece Jacole Miller. Two years later I re-introduced her to herself as Ms. Cole the nickname by which I call her. {Ms.} The prefix of respect and honor for which every woman should be addressed. GOD could not have given me a more beloved daughter and I am honored and proud beyond words to be given the privilege of writing this conclusion and to be called her father.

Allan J. Miller

Acknowledgments

To my Parents: EPITOME of parents. I couldn't live enough life times to express how grateful, thankful, and proud I am to be your child. The love that the two of you have for me is flawless. It's epic. It's wonderful. For your sacrifice, thank you! For your consistency, thank you! For your attention, thank you! For your responsibility, thank you! For your prayers, BLESS you! Never ever think that your rearing me was in vain. Even during the times when I put myself in tough situations, thank you for not coming to rescue me. You taught me how to rise when I fell. Your love and strength set the example for me to overcome any obstacle that I had to face. To be the child that belongs to both of you is gracious! I am because you are! You two are my FAVORITE people in the world. When I look at myself, I see both of you! Thank you for giving up the lives you had planned to birth me and bring me into the world. My love for you is deep. It's respectful. It's selfish. It's solid. It's sure. I am you! I love you!

To ALL of my Family and Friends: There are so many of you that I can't name everyone personally without writing another book! Thank you from the bottom of my heart for all of your love and support. Whether you know it or not, your prayers, text messages, calls, etc. during my college years really helped me stay sane. There is nothing like love from your own family.

To The McGruders: There really are no words to express my gratitude and appreciation for your love and support all of my life. Through my success and shortcomings you all were there and never changed. I love you from the bottom of my heart! To have the support that you provide is divine! I will always be grateful for you!!! THANK YOU! I love you!

To my cousins: Thank you for being the siblings I never had. Thank you for the love and support that you all have continued to show me. Thank you for the memories that we shared in our childhood. Thank you for always being a phone call away. The love I have for you all is deep and real. I love you all!

To my Stepmother: You are a beautiful soul! I have always known that I am a blessed woman, but God put the icing on the cake with you! I love you! I LOVE YOU! You being my daddy's wife is your assignment to him, but you being my stepmother is your purpose for me! The awesome thing about you is that not only are you my stepmother, you are also my friend! To be able to have those relationships with you is marvelous. Thank you for being you! Thank you for being more than I could ever imagine! Thank you for loving me as if I was your own! Thank you for your encouragement. Thank you for ALWAYS seeing the best in me! And thank you for always having the same thoughts as me! LOL ☺

To my Granny: Your presence in my life has been graceful. Thank you for planting seeds of excellence and greatness within me. Thank you for tough love. The standard that you set for me has been pivotal to my being. Your love has sustained me during hard and lonely times. Your tenacity has made me strong and tough against the enemy. Your prayers have kept me strong. I pray and plead to God that I am half the woman that you are! I love you from my soul. All of the times that I spent with you growing up as a child really made an impact on me. You have been the best grandmother, partner in love, ride or die (lol) that I could ever ask for. Honestly, I don't know what my life would be like without you. Your presence in my life has given me power. Thank you! I love you!

To Mrs. Debra Kiel: Thank you for being and incredible woman. During a detrimental time in my life dealing with health issues that my mother faced, your presence played a significant role and is part of the reason that I am the woman that I am today. The love you provided is a pure reflection of Jesus' heart. Thank you for your encouragement, nurturing, and respect that you had for my mother and me. I am forever grateful for you and the example you set. Your purpose for me was greater during the time your son and I were dating and I thank God that you were the woman He placed in my life during that time. Your standard as a wife, mother and friend has made a lasting impression on me. I love you always!

To the Pregnancy Care Center Stephenville, Texas: Thank you for being a reflection of Christ's heart. Even though I made my decision, you reminded me of the love that Jesus has for us. For your prayers and encouragement on that day, I am forever grateful!

To Mrs. Crystal Derrick: For your heart, thank you. For your wisdom, thank you. Your strength and faithfulness is admirable! There were many days that I drew from your strength and you were not aware. Thank you for ALWAYS spreading the love of Jesus. We were employed at the same place, but we were on divine assignment for one another as well. A true friend and sister you have always been to me. I love you.

To my sisters: Markesha, Chuntai, Ruqayyah, and Siobhan, thank you all for filling the void of not having biological sisters. Through it ALL you ladies have been there and I am grateful. I never thought that I would have the opportunity to call someone my sister. I know that God TRULY loves me because if I had the opportunity to design you all myself, I would do it the way that you already are and God knew that! Your friendship means so much to me and I will always cherish it! Chuntai and Ruqayyah-Anytime I need a laugh I always think about our times growing up together, sleeping in until four o'clock, using the shoestring to tie the bumper back on to the car, and eating nachos ALL the time. Markesha-to be able to have someone that you can tell all your secrets, the good and the bad and to know that they are safe is a rare treasure! You are a rare friend and I am so glad that you are all mine!

All of our fun times at TVCC, TSU, and random moments sitting in the car for hours in the parking lot are enough to give me laughs for the rest of my life. It is an honor to be your best friend and, I thank God for you and your family! Siobhan- A lady of grace! God knew EXACTLY what He was doing when He allowed us to cross paths. Your presence in my life has been epic! Someone that I am able to share as well as receive the word of God is a true gift from heaven. I am blessed that God has given you to me because at this point of my life, your love, wisdom, and presence has made a lasting impression on me. I have always wanted a big sister and God gave me you! Ladies, when the bible says that a true friend sticks closer than a brother that is definition of you! From the depths of my soul, I love you all! Thank you all for putting up with me and my attitude, stubbornness, and appetite! LOL…I love you sisters!

www.ingramcontent.com/pod-product-compliance
Lightning Source LLC
Chambersburg PA
CBHW072100290426
44110CB00014B/1756